Early Reading Intervention

Part 2

Student Activity Book 2

PEARSON

Scott Foresman

scottforesman.com

Editorial Offices: Glenview, Illinois • Parsippany, New Jersey • New York, New York
Sales Offices: Boston, Massachusetts • Duluth, Georgia • Glenview, Illinois
Coppell, Texas • Sacramento, California • Mesa, Arizona

ISBN: 0-328-26051-7

16 V095 15 14 13

Table of Contents

Name _____

Writer's Warm-Up

b   b

b   b   •   • | •   •

a   •   t   •

f   •   r   •

o   •   c   •

Activity 5

5

Writer's Warm-Up

b b

b b |

a •   s •

l •   m •

o •   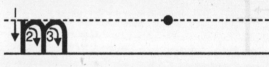 r •

© Pearson Education, Inc.

Name _____

Jack and the Beanstalk

Name _____

First and Last Sounds

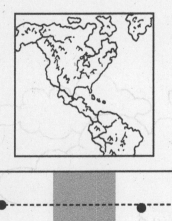

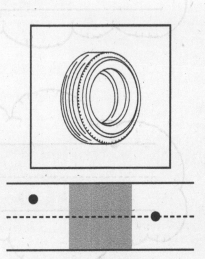

Activity 7

8

Name _____

Writer's Warm-Up

b

c

f

m

l

r

t

a

d

o

s

p

Activity 5

9

Tic-Tac-Toe

1

l		p
r		b
m		s

4

p		m
f		t
b		p

2

r		b
c		t
s		l

5

b		p
s		l
r		t

3

m		d
b		s
l		p

6

p		r
r		p
f		d

Name _____

Writer's Warm-Up

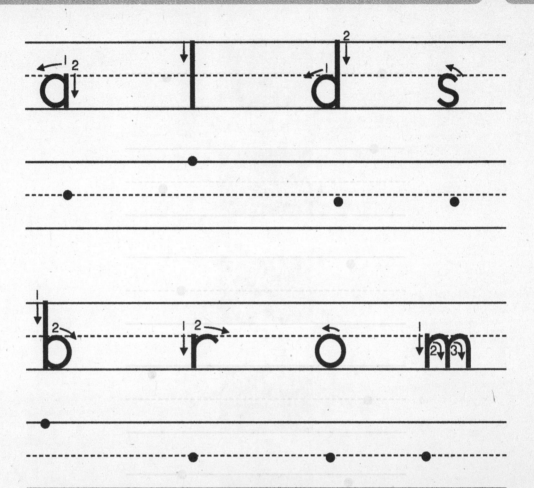

Activity 5

Word Writing Game

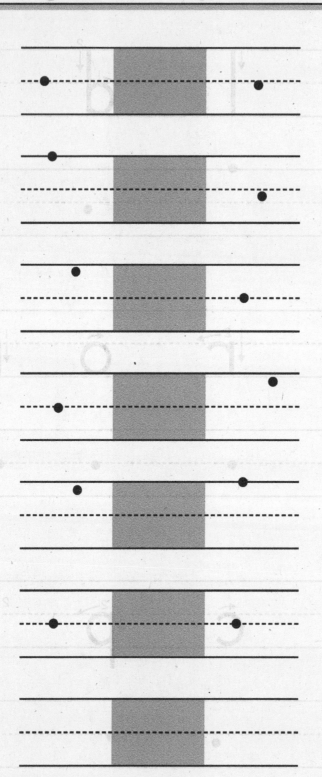

Name _____

Letter Mission

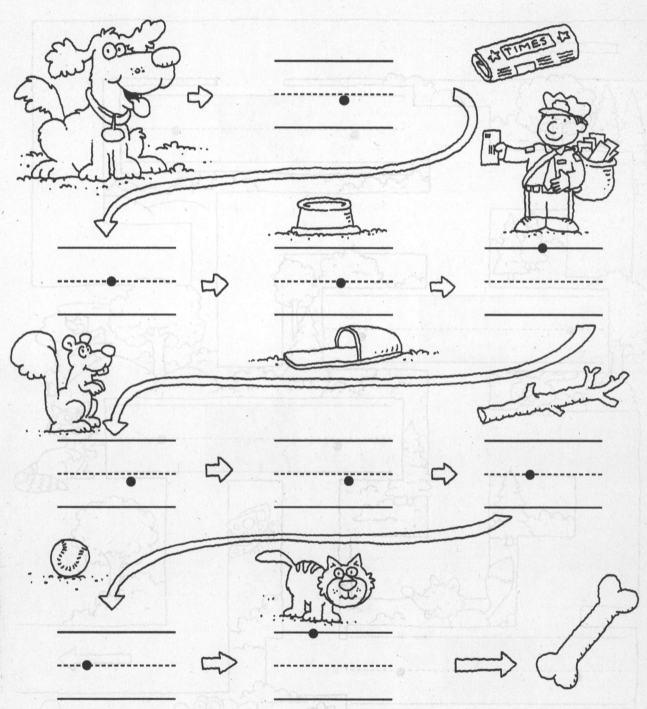

Name _____

Word Maze

Lesson
48

14

Activity 7

Name _____

Writer's Warm-Up

Lesson

49

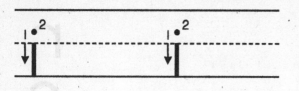

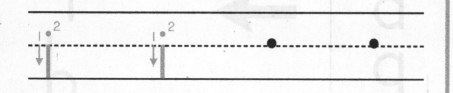

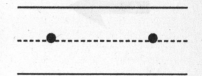

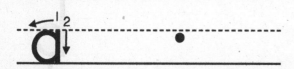

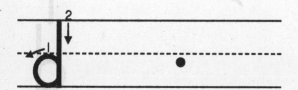

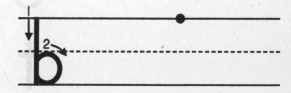

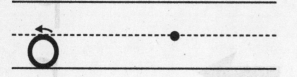

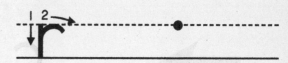

© Pearson Education, Inc.

Activity 5

15

Letter Tag

→ | t
b
p

→ | r
f
d

→ | b
c
t

→ | b
l
d

→ | r
c
t

→ | p
r
d

Name _____

Writer's Warm-Up

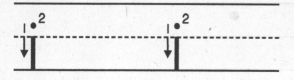

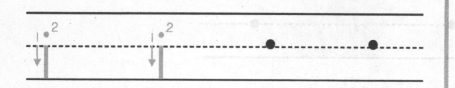
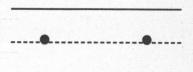

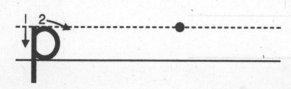
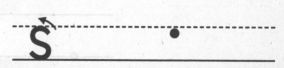

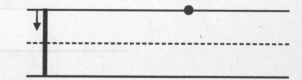

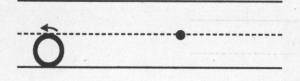
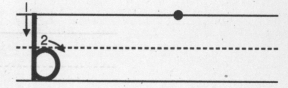

Activity 5

17

Rhyme Time

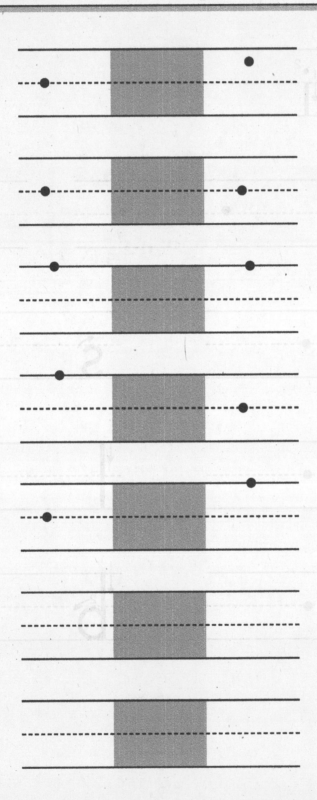

Name _____

Jack and the Beanstalk

Writer's Warm-Up

b

t

c

a

f

d

l

o

i

s

r

p

© Pearson Education, Inc.

Name _____

Writer's Warm-Up

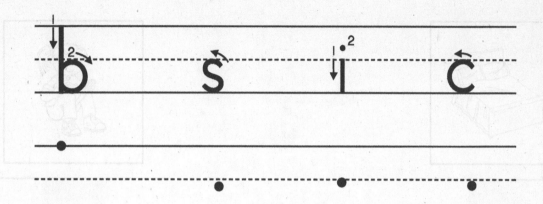

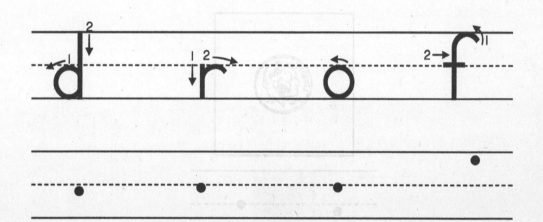

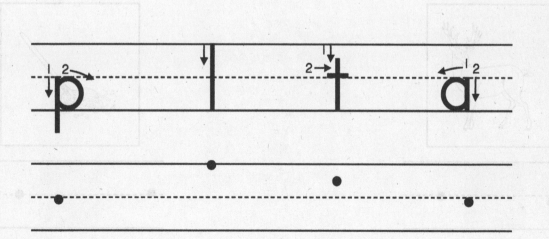

First and Last Sounds

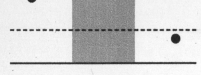

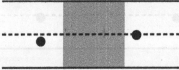

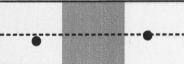

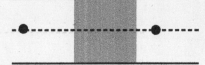

Treasure Hunt

Tic-Tac-Toe

1

c		p
t		b
m		l

4

d		r
l		t
t		b

2

c		s
l		p
t		b

5

d		p
c		t
b		l

3

t		s
l		t
p		d

6

d		m
c		f
b		t

Name _____

Writer's Warm-Up

n   n

n   n   •   •   │   •   •

a   •   s   •

d   •   i   •

o   •   r   •

b   •

Name _____

Word Maze

Lesson

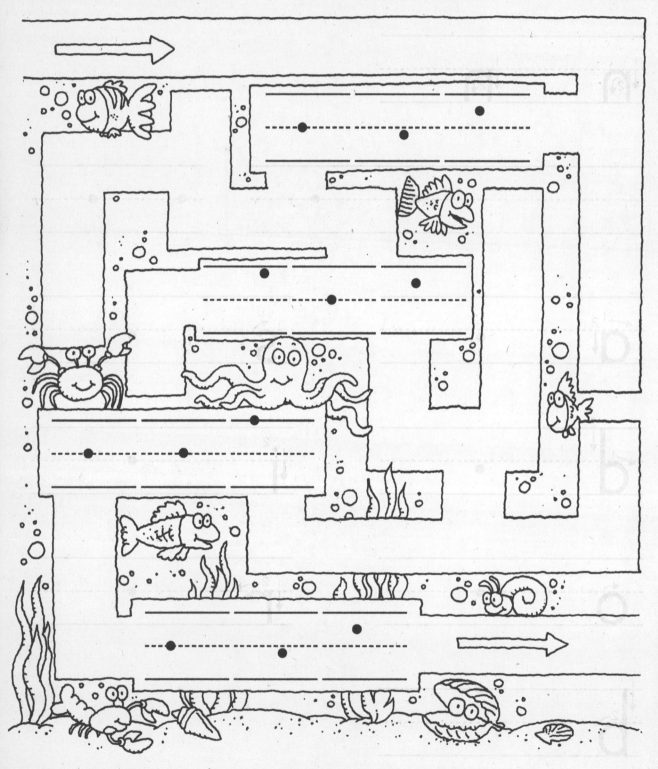

© Pearson Education, Inc.

Activity 7

Name _____

Writer's Warm-Up

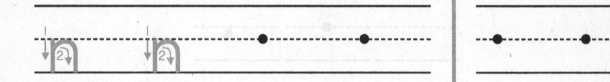

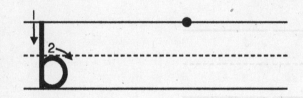

Activity 5

27

Word Writing Game

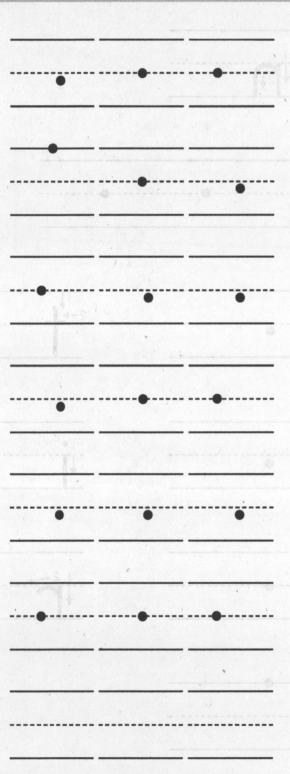

Activity 7

Word Race

Writer's Warm-Up

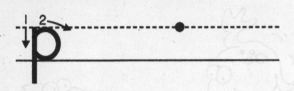

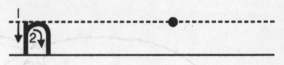

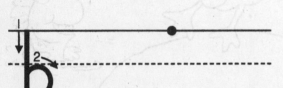

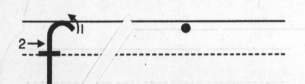

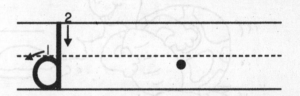

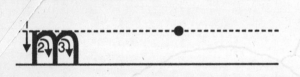

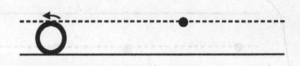

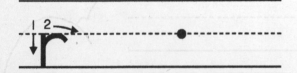

Activity 5

30

Writer's Warm-Up

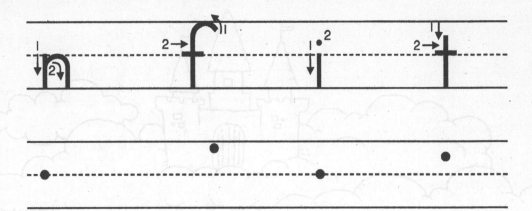

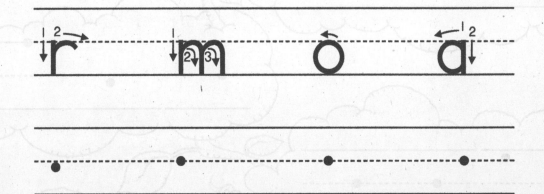

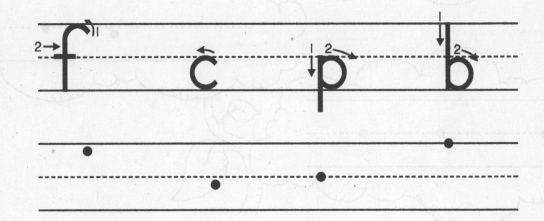

Jack and the Beanstalk

Name _____

Treasure Hunt

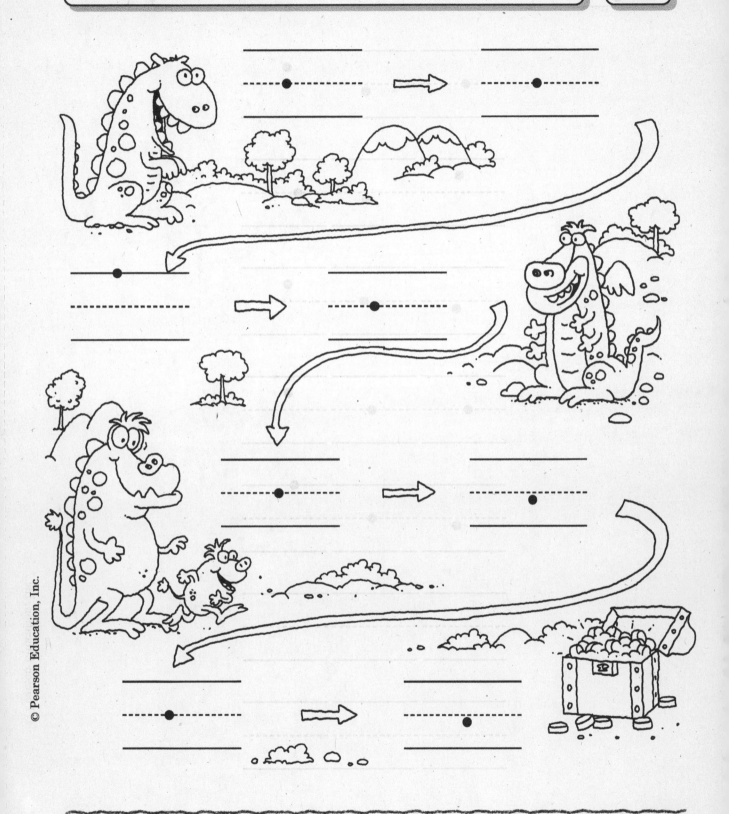

Activity 5

33

Rhyme Time

Name _____

Writer's Warm-Up

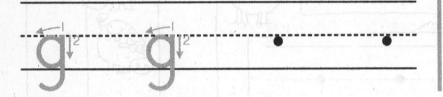

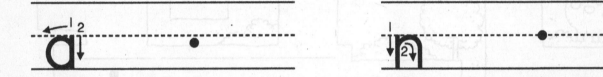

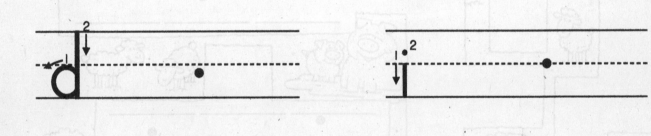

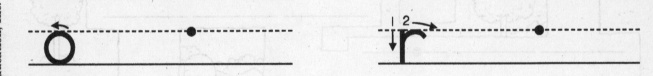

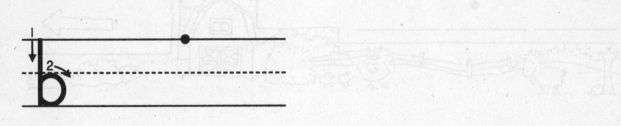

Word Maze

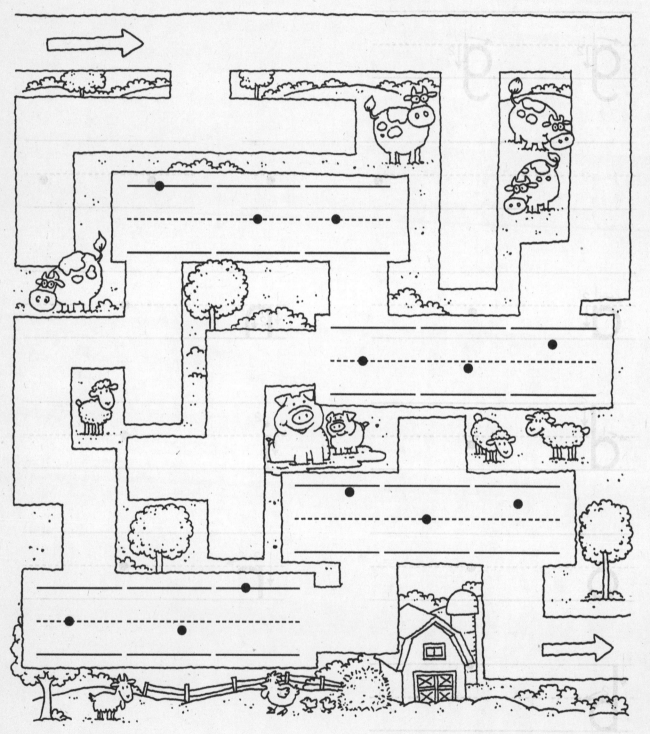

Activity 7

Writer's Warm-Up

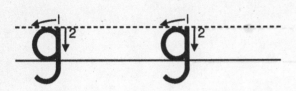

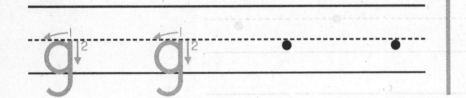

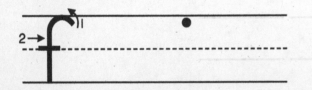

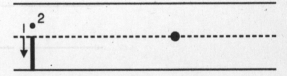

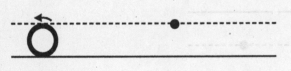

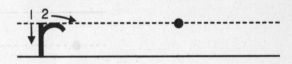

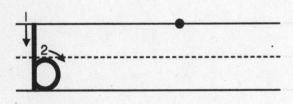

Word Writing Game

Word Race

Name _____

Writer's Warm-Up

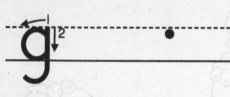

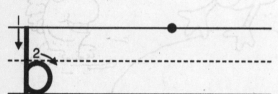

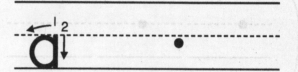

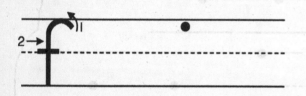

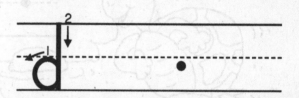

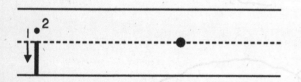

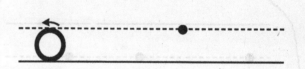

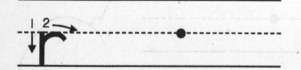

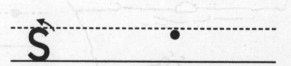

Activity 5

Name _____

Writer's Warm-Up

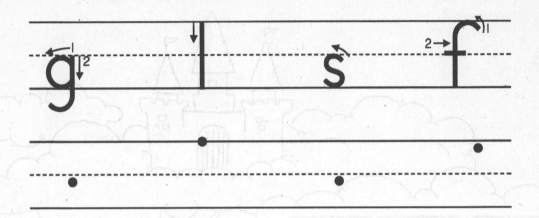

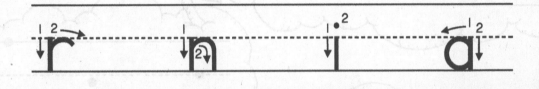

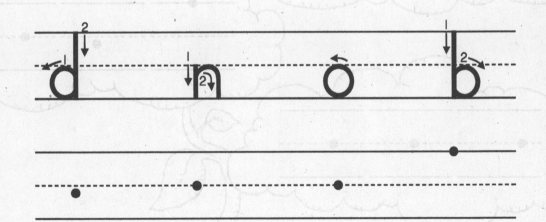

Activity 5

41

Name _____

Jack and the Beanstalk

Lesson **65**

Activity 7

Name _____

Treasure Hunt

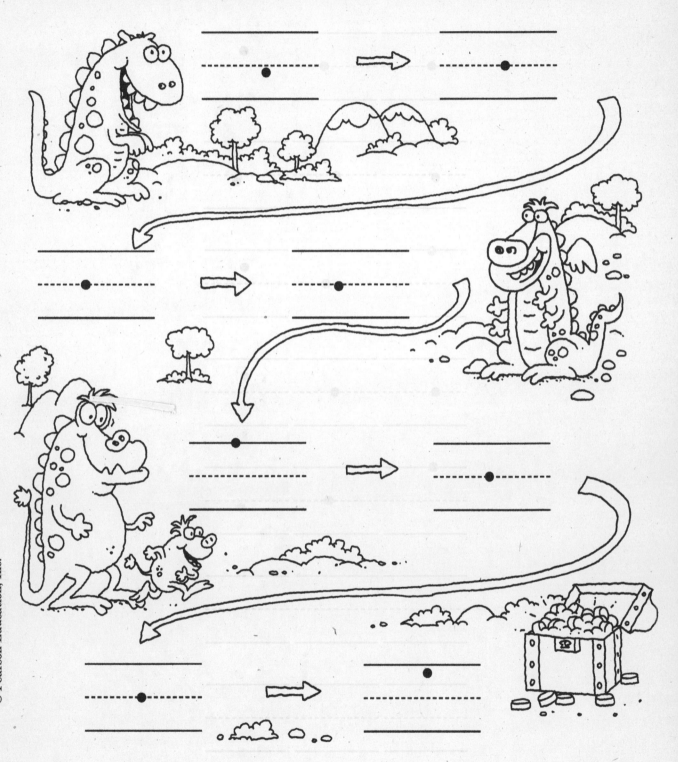

Name _____

Rhyme Time

Activity 7
44

Writer's Warm-Up

u u

u u

a n

g i

o r

b

© Pearson Education, Inc.

Name _____

Word Maze

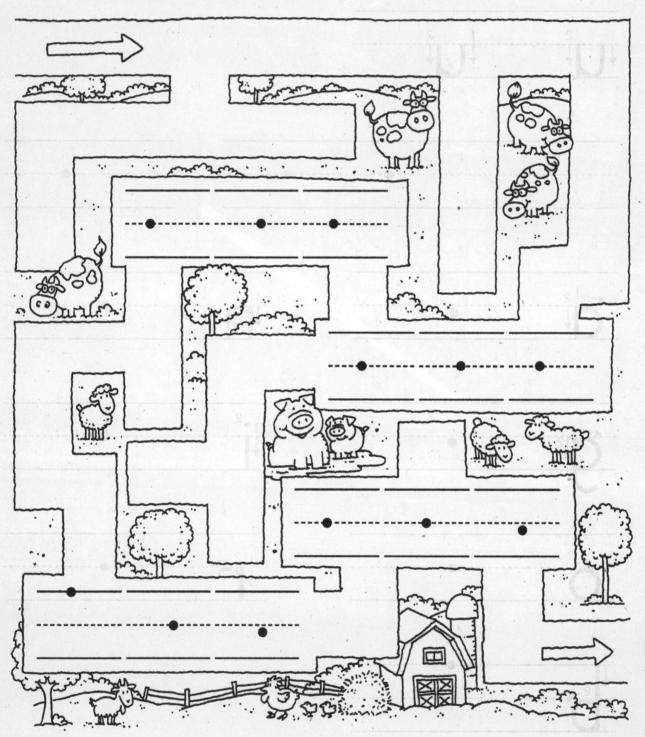

Name _____

Writer's Warm-Up

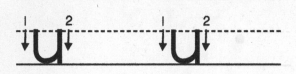

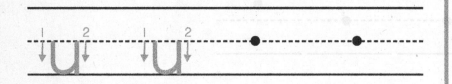
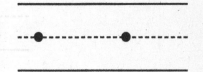

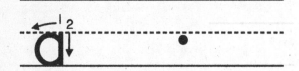

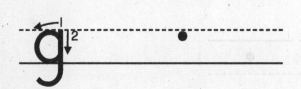
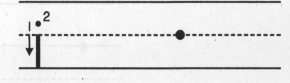

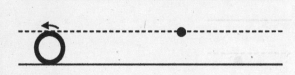
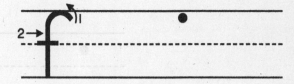

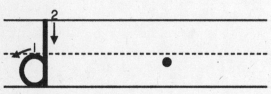

Activity 5

Name _____

Word Writing Game

Word Race

Name _____

Writer's Warm-Up

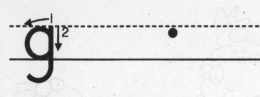

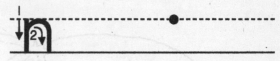

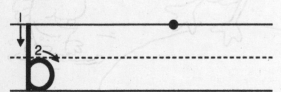

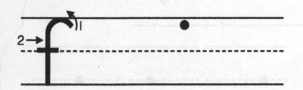

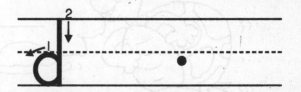

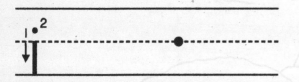

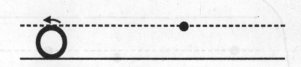

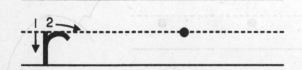

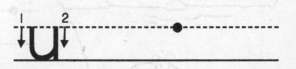

Activity 5

50

Name _____

Writer's Warm-Up

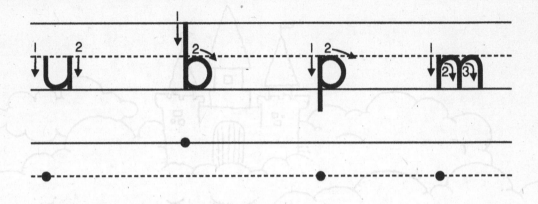

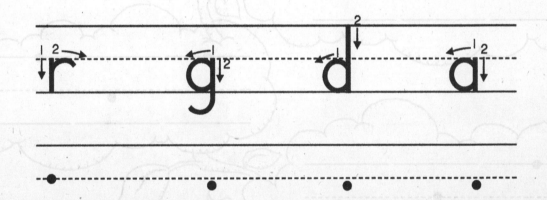

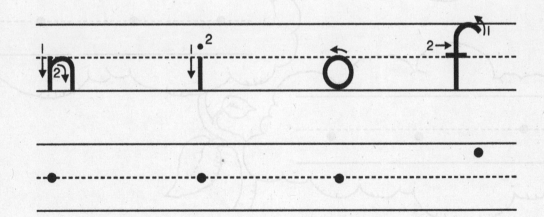

Name _____

Jack and the Beanstalk

Activity 7

52

Name _____

Lesson
72

Treasure Hunt

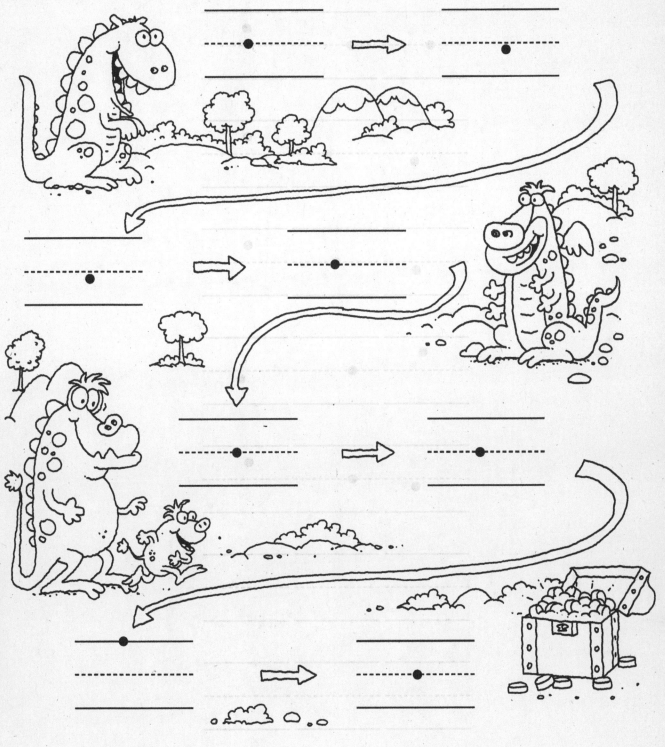

© Pearson Education, Inc.

Activity 5

53

Name _____

Rhyme Time

Activity 7